CONTENTS

STORIES OF THE CIVIL RIGHTS MOVEMENT

THE LITTLE ROCK NINE

by Carla Mooney

Content Consultant
David A. Canton, PhD
Associate Professor of History
Connecticut College

Core Library

An Imprint of Abdo Publishing
abdopublishing.com

abdopublishing.com

Published by Abdo Publishing, a division of ABDO, PO Box 398166, Minneapolis,
Minnesota 55439. Copyright © 2016 by Abdo Consulting Group, Inc. International
copyrights reserved in all countries. No part of this book may be reproduced in any form
without written permission from the publisher. Core Library™ is a trademark and logo of
Abdo Publishing.

Printed in the United States of America, North Mankato, Minnesota

032015
092015

**THIS BOOK CONTAINS
RECYCLED MATERIALS**

Cover Photo: AP Images
Interior Photos: AP Images, 1, 4, 15, 21, 27, 30; William P. Straeter/AP Images, 6, 45;
Bettmann/Corbis, 8, 10, 39, 43; North Wind Picture Archives, 12; Ferd Kaufman/AP
Images, 18; Corbis, 24; Underwood Archives/Universal Images Group/Newscom, 33;
Danny Johnston/AP Images, 36

Editor: Jon Westmark
Series Designer: Becky Daum

Library of Congress Control Number: 2015931186

Cataloging-in-Publication Data
Mooney, Carla.
The Little Rock Nine / Carla Mooney.
    p. cm. -- (Stories of the civil rights movement)
Includes bibliographical references and index.
ISBN 978-1-62403-880-8
1. School integration--Arkansas--Little Rock--History--20th century--Juvenile literature.
2. African American students--Arkansas--Little Rock--History--20th century--Juvenile
literature. 3. Central High School (Little Rock, Ark.)--History--20th century--Juvenile
literature. 4. Little Rock (Ark.)--Race relations--Juvenile literature.   I. Title.
379.2--dc23
                                                                    2015931186

CHAPTER ONE

WALKING WITH COURAGE

On the morning of September 4, 1957, 15-year-old Elizabeth Eckford got ready for school. She carefully put on a new dress. She had made it herself. Her mother helped her straighten and curl her hair. Elizabeth wanted to look nice on the first day of school. She knew this was no ordinary first day. She had applied and been selected to attend Central High School in Little Rock,

National Guardsmen snap to attention outside Central High School on September 3, 1957, the day before classes began.

Hundreds gather outside Central High School to protest against integration.

Arkansas, along with eight other African-American students. Until then the schools in Little Rock were segregated. The African-American school in Little Rock was not as good as the school for whites because the African-American school got less money from the city. These nine students would be the first African-American students to go to Central High. Many people in Little Rock and around the country were upset. They did not want African-American and white students to go to the same school.

As Elizabeth ate breakfast, a television news reporter described large crowds gathering around

Central High. Elizabeth's mother told her to turn it off. She warned Elizabeth that people might say bad things to her on her way into school. She said Elizabeth should pretend not to hear them.

Elizabeth rode a city bus to within two blocks of Central High. When she got off the bus, she noticed that there were many cars and people on the street. As she got closer to the school, Elizabeth saw Arkansas National Guard soldiers. She saw the soldiers allow white students into the

CIVIL RIGHTS VOICES
Elizabeth Eckford

I turned back to the guards but their faces told me I wouldn't get help from them. Then I looked down the block and saw a bench at the bus stop. I thought, "If I can only get there, I will be safe."

Elizabeth Eckford became a lasting image of the fight for school integration. A picture of her walking alone as she tried to enter Central High was printed around the world. All of Little Rock's high schools were closed the next year, so Eckford did not graduate from Central High School. She joined the US Army and earned a certificate equal to a high school degree. She later earned a history degree from Central State University in Wilberforce, Ohio.

Elizabeth Eckford is directed away from Central High School. She was the first of the nine African-American students to arrive.

school building. She thought the guards were there to help her get into the school safely.

Elizabeth approached the guards as she had seen the white students do. But the National Guardsmen stopped her. They told her to move to the other side of the street.

Elizabeth walked farther down the line of guards. A crowd formed behind her. Her knees shook in fear. She tried to pass through the line again. The guards crossed their guns and blocked her.

Elizabeth kept walking down the street. People from the crowd followed her. Some yelled for her to be lynched. Many called her names. They shouted at her to go home. One woman spat in her face.

Elizabeth walked to the bus stop to go home. She did not know what else to do. She sat there a long time before the bus came. A white woman named Grace Lorch stayed with Elizabeth. The crowd screamed insults and death threats. Lorch

Grace Lorch

Grace Lorch was one of the few who helped Elizabeth Eckford as she retreated from the angry mob. Lorch was a white woman who supported integration. She went to Central High that day to support the African-American students. Her husband Lee was an official with the Arkansas chapter of the National Association for the Advancement of Colored People (NAACP). He accompanied some of the African-American students to school. The Lorchs' actions made their family a target. Someone burned crosses on their lawn. Their daughter was bullied at school. Someone even put dynamite in their garage.

A group of reporters surrounds Elizabeth as she walks away from Central High School.

helped Elizabeth board a bus that would take her away from the mob.

Elizabeth and the other African-American students were all turned away from Central High that day. They would eventually be allowed to attend classes at the school. They would face threats, insults, and violence over the course of the school year. But these young students refused to back down. They wanted the same opportunities as their white classmates. And civil rights leaders across the United States supported the cause. They hoped it would lead to a better country for everyone. The students became known as the Little Rock Nine. With courage and grace, they captured the attention of the world and helped bring long-lasting change to the US school system.

EXPLORE ONLINE

Chapter One discusses Elizabeth Eckford's experience on her first day of school at Central High. The website below explores Carlotta Walls' experience on her first day. Walls was also a member of the Little Rock Nine. As you know, every source is different. What information does the website give about the first day of school for the nine African-American students? How is the information from the website the same as the information in Chapter One? What new information did you learn from the website?

Q+A: The Youngest of the Little Rock Nine Talks About Her First Day of School

mycorelibrary.com/the-little-rock-nine

CHAPTER TWO

A LONG HISTORY OF RACIAL OPPRESSION

Segregated schools were one part of a long history of racial oppression in the United States. Starting in the 1600s, white colonists brought people from Africa to work as slaves. Slavery existed throughout the country. In rural areas, many were forced to work on large plantations. Slaves were the property of their owners. Slave owners could buy and sell slaves as they wished.

Slaves on plantations were often forced to do hard work from sunrise until sunset.

Opposing Slavery

Enslaved Africans believed slavery was wrong. Some white Americans also believed it was wrong. These people tried to get the federal government to abolish slavery in the 1800s. Many people in the southern states did not support this. The disagreement between states led to the Civil War (1861–1865). The southern states lost the war. Slavery was abolished throughout the country.

Constitutional Changes

In 1865 Congress passed the Thirteenth Amendment to the US Constitution. The amendment abolished slavery throughout the United States. Congress then passed two more amendments that gave rights to the former slaves. The Fourteenth Amendment (1868) granted citizenship and equal protection under the law to every person born or naturalized in the United States. The Fifteenth Amendment (1870) gave African-American men the right to vote.

Segregation and Jim Crow Laws

Many white southerners were angry that they were forced to abolish slavery.

A police officer sets a segregation sign outside a railroad depot in Jackson, Mississippi.

They did not see African Americans as equal citizens. They helped pass laws that made it hard for African Americans to be treated equally to whites. The laws were called Jim Crow laws. Jim Crow laws separated people based on race.

Plessy v. Ferguson

In 1896 an African-American man named Homer Plessy challenged a Jim Crow law. He refused to move out of a white-only railroad car and was arrested. Plessy sued the railroad company. He claimed that segregation was illegal. His case went to the Supreme Court. In *Plessy v. Ferguson*, the court ruled that separation by race was constitutional as long as equal facilities were available to all. This decision led to the idea of "separate but equal" segregation.

In reality things were not equal. Often the facilities for whites were far better than those used by African Americans.

Schools were one example. African-American schools were usually more crowded than white-only schools. The school buildings often needed repairs. Many did not have indoor plumbing. These schools also did not have the same equipment and books that white schools did.

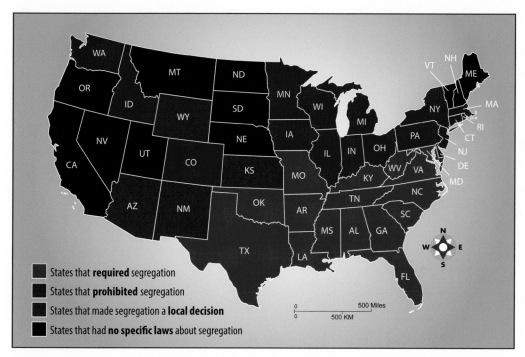

States that **required** segregation
States that **prohibited** segregation
States that made segregation a **local decision**
States that had **no specific laws** about segregation

Segregation in Education before 1954

Segregation in schools varied from state to state before the Supreme Court's ruling in *Brown v. Board of Education*. What do you notice about the different US regions? How does the map help you understand the significance of the Supreme Court's decision?

Brown v. Board of Education

In the 1950s, several court cases challenged segregation in schools. Attorneys argued that separate schools were not equal. The US Supreme Court ruled in *Brown v. Board of Education* that segregation of US public schools was unconstitutional on May 17, 1954.

NEW WEST END
HIGH SCHOOL
"H" AND McKINLEY STREETS
LITTLE ROCK, ARKANSAS

CAPACITY 1000 PUPILS
37 CLASSROOMS · COMPLETE FACILITIES

DATE OF CONTRACT	APRIL 18, 1956
DATE OF OCCUPANCY	ESTIMATED, SEPT. 1957
COST OF SITE	$86,650.00
COST OF BUILDING, INCLUDING FEES	$949,989.00 (ESTIMATE)
SQUARE FOOT COST	$ 9.87
...NITURE ...ENT	NO ESTIMATE
...S AND ...MENT	NO ESTIMATE
	NOT AVAILABLE

CHAPTER THREE

THE BATTLE FOR INTEGRATION IN LITTLE ROCK

In 1954 the Little Rock school board announced that it would follow the Supreme Court's order to desegregate schools. Little Rock school superintendent Virgil Blossom developed a plan for the district. The Blossom Plan called for the Little Rock schools to integrate in three parts. First a few African-American students would attend the all-white Central High School in 1957. The district's junior high

Superintendent Virgil Blossom looks over the integration plan for the Little Rock public schools. He had worked on the plan for three years.

Who Would Be First?

Civil rights activist Daisy Bates and the NAACP worked to find students who wanted to attend Central. The school board screened interested students. It approved 17 to transfer. The students went to counseling sessions in the weeks before school started. They learned what to expect at Central. They also learned how to handle difficult situations and classmates. Eight of the 17 students withdrew before school started. The remaining students became the Little Rock Nine. They were Minnijean Brown, Elizabeth Eckford, Ernest Green, Thelma Mothershed, Melba Pattillo, Gloria Ray, Terrence Roberts, Jefferson Thomas, and Carlotta Walls.

schools would integrate by 1960. The elementary schools would integrate by 1963.

Some people thought the Blossom Plan was too slow. Civil rights activist Daisy Bates and other members of the National Association for the Advancement of Colored People (NAACP) organized students who wanted to go to white schools. But school officials did not let the students register.

In February 1956, Bates and the NAACP filed a lawsuit on behalf of

Daisy Bates and others from the NAACP carefully went over each application to make sure the students were prepared for what might occur.

the students against the Little Rock School District. A federal judge dismissed the lawsuit. He said that Little Rock's Blossom Plan followed the Supreme Court's ruling. The NAACP brought the case to another court, but that judge agreed with the first.

Opposition

Many white people in Little Rock and across the South opposed school integration. They were upset the federal government was making them change state and local laws. The Capital Citizens' Council in Little Rock urged the public to resist integration. It bought newspaper ads and held public rallies. The council asked people to write letters and call Arkansas Governor Orval Faubus and urge him to stop integration.

The Mother's League of Central High also petitioned the Arkansas governor to stop desegregation at Central. In August 1957, the group tried to get a court order

	Whites	African Americans			Whites	African Americans
Alabama	$1,158	$661		Missouri	$1,397	$1,590*
Arkansas	$942	$555		North Carolina	$1,380	$1,249
Delaware	$1,953	$1,814		Oklahoma	$1,428	$1,438
Florida	$1,530	$970		South Carolina	$1,203	$615
Georgia	$1,123	$515		Tennessee	$1,071	$1,010
Louisiana	$1,683	$828		Texas	$1,395	$946
Maryland	$2,085	$2,002		Virginia	$1,364	$1,129
Mississippi	$1,107	$342		District of Columbia	$2,610	$2,610

*Higher average salary due mainly to the fact that African-American schools were highly concentrated in cities where all salaries were higher.

Unequal Opportunity: Comparison of Teacher Salaries

A report ordered by President Harry Truman in 1946 found that African-American students were at a disadvantage compared to white students in the South. One measure the report looked at was teacher salaries. How does this chart support the idea that African-American students in segregated Southern schools were at a disadvantage?

to stop the integration plan. At first a judge granted the injunction to stop African-American students from attending Central. The next day, federal district judge Ronald Davies overturned the injunction. He ordered the Little Rock School Board to start integrated classes on September 4.

CHAPTER FOUR

THE LITTLE ROCK NINE

Tensions increased in Little Rock as the 1957 school year approached. On September 2, Arkansas Governor Orval Faubus claimed he needed to keep the peace. He called in the Arkansas National Guard. Faubus ordered them to stop any African-American students from entering Central High School.

Soldiers surround the school to make sure the Little Rock Nine cannot enter.

Carlotta Walls Lanier

You can overcome adversity if you know you are doing the right thing.

Carlotta Walls was the youngest member of the Little Rock Nine. She chose to go to Central High because she wanted to get the best education she could. She was harassed daily at Central. Still she concentrated on her schoolwork. She graduated from Central in 1960. Carlotta went on to start a real estate company after college. She is the president of the Little Rock Nine Foundation, a scholarship organization that works to give access to education for African-American students.

Arrival at Central

The Little Rock Nine arrived at Central High School on September 4. Daisy Bates had called the students and arranged for them to walk to school together. Elizabeth Eckford arrived on her own because her family did not have a telephone. As the rest of the Nine approached the school, the mob closed in on them. The students tried to pass. But the National Guard turned them away.

Reporter Alex Wilson is shoved by an angry mob outside Central High School on September 23, 1957.

Tensions Rise

White protesters continued to gather around the school. On September 20, Judge Davies ordered the governor to remove the National Guard from Central. Governor Faubus withdrew the troops.

On Monday, September 23, more than 1,000 people gathered outside Central. The Little Rock

Nine entered through a side door. By lunchtime the crowd was getting out of control. The police feared the crowd might go into the school and hurt the African-American students. The nine students were removed from the school.

Presidential Meeting

On September 14, 1957, President Eisenhower met with Governor Faubus. Eisenhower wanted the governor to find a solution to the crisis. The two men met at Eisenhower's vacation home in Rhode Island. They discussed the situation in Little Rock but could not come to an agreement. Faubus did not remove the Arkansas National Guard.

Federal Troops Arrive

On September 24, President Dwight D. Eisenhower sent more than 1,000 troops from the US Army's 101st Airborne Division to keep the peace. The soldiers escorted the Little Rock Nine into Central High the next day. The nine students finally attended their first full day of class.

President Eisenhower sent US Army troops to Little Rock to make sure the African-American students were allowed to enter Central. The parents of the Little Rock Nine thanked Eisenhower in this passage from a telegram:

> We the parents of nine negro children enrolled at Little Rock Central High School want you to know that your action in safe guarding their rights have strengthened our faith in democracy. Now as never before we have an abiding feeling of belonging and purposefulness. We believe that freedom and equality with which all men are endowed at birth can be maintained only through freedom and equality of opportunity. . . . We believe that the degree to which people everywhere realize and accept this concept will determine in a large measure America's true growth and true greatness. You have demonstrated admirably to us the nation and the world how profoundly you believe in this concept. For this we are deeply grateful. . . .
>
> Source: Parents of the Little Rock Nine. Letter to President Eisenhower. October 1, 1957. DDE Records as President, Eisenhower Presidential Library, Abilene, KS.

What's the Big Idea?
Read the primary source text carefully. What is its main idea? How is the main idea supported by details? Name two or three details used to support the main idea in this text.

CHAPTER FIVE

CONTINUING CHALLENGES

Inside Central High School, soldiers escorted the African-American students to classes. But the Little Rock Nine endured daily abuse, particularly in bathrooms and locker rooms where the guards were not allowed to go. Sometimes white students yelled threats and insults at them. Other times white students made and passed out insulting flyers. Sometimes the attacks were physical. The nine

Seven of the Little Rock Nine students are escorted onto campus on October 15, 1957.

Terrence Roberts

And even with the guards present, it was possible for kids to simply race up behind us and push, shove, kick, spit or whatever, and then take off running. So they devised many, many ways. The main goal was to try to force us out.

Terrence Roberts was one of the Little Rock Nine. He endured the 1957–1958 school year at Central High. He left Little Rock in 1958 and finished high school in California. He went on to earn a doctorate degree in psychology. He has worked in a mental health hospital, taught psychology, and started his own business. He regularly speaks to groups about the events at Central High School.

students were regularly shoved, kicked, hit, or spit upon. Other students broke into and vandalized their lockers. Often school officials did little to stop the attacks. No one was punished if a teacher did not see it.

Some violence was serious. Terrence Roberts was hit on the head with a combination lock. Gloria Ray was pushed down a flight of stairs. One student threw acid in Melba Pattillo's face. Several

National Guard troops break up a group of students outside Central. Approximately 75 students walked out of school on October 3, 1957, to protest integration.

white students also hanged, stabbed, and burned an African-American effigy near the school.

Graduation

Despite the challenges, eight of the nine African-American students finished the school year. On May 25, 1958, senior Ernest Green became the first African American to graduate from Central High.

In September 1958, Governor Faubus closed all of Little Rock's high schools for the year.

Expelled

In February 1958, Minnijean Brown had reached her limit. She had endured daily threats, insults, and physical attacks. She was also upset that she was not allowed to participate in school activities. One day she dropped a bowl of chili on a white student who had been taunting her. She was expelled from Central. The white students who had tormented her were not. Brown finished high school in New York City.

Some of the African-American students moved or took courses through the mail. Only two returned to Central when it reopened in 1959.

Melba Pattillo described in a diary entry the daily harassment she faced at Central High as one of the Little Rock Nine:

February 18, 1958

A red-haired, freckle-faced girl, the one who taunts me in homeroom, keeps trailing me in the hallway between classes. Today she spit on me, then slapped me. Later in the day as I came around a corner, she tripped me so that I fell down a flight of stairs. I picked myself up to face a group of boys who then chased me up the stairs. When I told a school official about it, he said she was from a good family and would never do such a thing and I needed a teacher to witness these incidents if he were going to take any action. He asked me what did I expect when I came to a place where I knew I wasn't welcome.

Source: Melba Pattillo Beals. Warriors Don't Cry. New York: Simon Pulse, 2007. Print. 169.

Back It Up

The author of this passage is using evidence to support a point. Write a paragraph describing the point the author is making. Then write down two or three pieces of evidence the author uses to make the point.

CHAPTER SIX

IMPACT OF THE LITTLE ROCK NINE

On September 25, 2007, the Little Rock Nine returned to Central High School. Fifty years earlier, they had walked through an angry mob that shouted insults. This time a crowd of 5,000 cheered and asked for autographs.

Achieving Goals

The nine students spread around the country after the 1957 crisis. They went on to lead successful lives.

Elizabeth Eckford walks by a statue of herself. A monument honoring the Little Rock Nine sits outside the Arkansas state capitol.

Awards and Honors

The nine students received several awards for their role in the struggle for civil rights. In 1958 the NAACP awarded the Spingarn Medal to Daisy Bates and the Little Rock Nine. This medal is awarded each year for outstanding achievement by an African American.

In 1999 the US Congress awarded the Little Rock Nine the US Congressional Gold Medal. This is the highest honor a US civilian can earn. It is awarded for service to the country.

Several earned college and graduate degrees. They worked in a variety of fields, including accounting, journalism, social work, teaching, and banking. Minnijean Brown worked as Deputy Assistant Secretary for Workforce Diversity under President Bill Clinton. Ernest Green became the Assistant Secretary of the Department of Labor under President Jimmy Carter.

Inspiring a Nation

The Little Rock Nine achieved more than desegregating Central High School. They became role models for the civil rights movement. The

The nine African-American students appeared in court to sign statements about the events at Central High School.

Brown v. Board of Education decision in 1954 marked the beginning of the civil rights movement for many people. The Little Rock Nine's effort to end school

CIVIL RIGHTS VOICES
Melba Pattillo

If one person is denied equality, we are all denied equality.

Melba Pattillo endured daily harassment at Central High as one of the Little Rock Nine. She finished the year at Central. When the school was closed the following year, she moved to Santa Rosa, California, to complete her senior year of high school. She earned a master's degree in journalism from Columbia University. She worked as a reporter for NBC. She also wrote a book about her experiences at Central High School, *Warriors Don't Cry*. The book has won several awards.

segregation inspired many others to stand up for equality.

The civil rights movement grew in the years after the students attended Central High School. Civil rights activists organized sit-ins and rallies. Martin Luther King Jr. inspired hundreds of thousands of people. Then the movement made a breakthrough. The US Congress passed the Civil Rights Act of 1964. It gave equal rights to all people regardless of race, color, religion, gender, or national origin. The act was later expanded to include disabled Americans, the elderly, and women in college athletics. Although the struggle against racism was not over in the United States, legal segregation was no longer allowed.

Today Central High School is a national historic site. The school still educates Little Rock students. It is fully integrated. Students of many races go to class together.

FURTHER EVIDENCE

There is a lot of information about the impact of the Little Rock Nine in Chapter Six. If you could pick out the main point of the chapter, what would it be? Find a few pieces of key evidence from the text that support the main point. Then explore the website below to learn even more about the Little Rock Nine's legacy. Find a quote from the website that supports the chapter's main point. Does the quote support an existing piece of evidence in the chapter? Or does it add a new piece of evidence?

Showdown in Little Rock
mycorelibrary.com/the-little-rock-nine

Elizabeth Eckford walks alone through a crowd of angry adults and students as she tries to enter Central High School. The white girl behind her, Hazel Bryan, yells a racial insult.

Date

September 4, 1957

Key Players

Elizabeth Eckford, Hazel Bryan

What Happened

The Arkansas National Guard blocked Elizabeth from entering Central High that day. A few weeks later, Elizabeth and the other members of the Little Rock Nine began attending classes at the school.

Impact

This photo was published around the country and the world. The anger captured in Hazel Bryan's face surprised and shocked many. It focused the nation's attention on the crisis in Little Rock and the barriers that African Americans faced.

STOP AND THINK

Say What?

Find five words in this book that you have never seen or heard before. Find each word in a dictionary and read the definition. Rewrite the word's definition in your own words. Then use each word in a sentence.

Why Do I Care?

Think about two or three ways the struggles and actions of the Little Rock Nine connect to your own life. Give examples of parts of your life that have a connection to the Little Rock Nine.

You Are There

Imagine that you lived in Little Rock, Arkansas, in 1957. Write 300 words describing your life. What do you see happening in your town? How has your school changed? What are your neighbors saying?

Surprise Me

Think about what you learned from this book. Can you name the two or three facts in this book that you found most surprising? Write a short paragraph about each, describing what you found surprising and why.

GLOSSARY

abolish
to formally put an end to a practice, such as slavery

activist
a person who campaigns for social change

desegregate
to end a policy of racial separation

effigy
a roughly made model of a person

injunction
a court order that restrains a person from beginning or continuing an action

integrate
to make open to all cultures and races

lynch
to kill someone without a legal trial

naturalized
to become a citizen of a country

oppression
prolonged cruel or unfair treatment

plantation
a large farm where crops are grown to be sold

segregate
to separate people according to race, sexual orientation, gender, or religious beliefs

unconstitutional
not in agreement with a constitution, particularly the US Constitution

LEARN MORE

Books

Beals, Melba Pattillo. *Warriors Don't Cry*. New York: Simon Pulse, 2007.

Poe, Marshall. *Little Rock Nine*. New York: Aladdin, 2008.

Walker, Paul Robert. *Remember Little Rock: The Time, the People, the Stories*. Washington, DC: National Geographic, 2009.

Websites

To learn more about Stories of the Civil Rights Movement, visit **booklinks.abdopublishing.com**. These links are routinely monitored and updated to provide the most current information available.

Visit **mycorelibrary.com** for free additional tools for teachers and students.

INDEX

ABOUT THE AUTHOR

Carla Mooney has written many books for young people. She loves learning about events in history. A graduate of the University of Pennsylvania, she lives in Pittsburgh, Pennsylvania, with her husband and three children.